Piety and Plum Porridge

BLINKING EYE PUBLISHING

BLINKING EYE PUBLISHING

First published 2005
by:
Blinking Eye Publishing
P.O. Box 549
North Shields, Tyne & Wear
NE30 2WT

ISBN: 0-9549036-3-3

for further information about Blinking Eye Publishing
please visit our website: www.blinking-eye.co.uk
or write to the above address.

Blinking Eye Publishing acknowledges
the financial assistance of
Arts Council England, North East

© Individual Authors 2005
© Blinking Eye Publishers

All rights reserved.
No part of this book may be reproduced,
stored in a retrieval system, or transmitted in any form,
or by any means, electronic, mechanical, photocopying,
recording or otherwise without prior
written permission from the publishers

Cover photography by Adam Lawrenson,
Forest Hall
Printed in Great Britain:
thenewprinthouse Ltd. North Shields.

Acknowledgements

Acknowledgements are due to the Arts Council England, North East for their financial support: also my friends and fellow poets for their continuous encouragement. Emma Holliday, for her painting of the Millennium Bridge (now in a private collection) which is used as the logo for Blinking Eye Publishing website. Also the support of the small presses: Other Poetry; Smiths Knoll; Sand; Partners; and Orbis. I acknowledge the poetry libraries and county libraries within the United Kingdom, and all websites that have linked me via their own websites, to help promote this worthy venture.

Jeanne Macdonald

Introduction

Piety and Plum Porridge is the second anthology published by Blinking Eye Publishing. The contributors include the winner of our 2005 poetry competition, A C Clarke; also the judge's three highly commended poets. As Editor, I have chosen the commended poets, whose poems, I believe, will give pleasure to readers.

The wide range of poetry in this anthology offers an enjoyable read, and I recommend this book not only to those of similar age (entrants must be over the age of fifty to enter the competition), but also to the younger reader.

In the summing up after his judgment of this competition WN Herbert, wrote:

'Poetry is not an exact science, it is an exact experience: as the advert has it, you know when you've been tangoed. To read a poem is to be thrown into proximity with another sensibility in a manner as intimate and yet distant as the tango, and I always measure the quality of any given poem by the breadth and depth of its effect. Did it startle and delight not just verbally, intellectually and emotionally, but in the instincts, where music and imagery collide in ways that resonate long after the reading is done?'

Jeanne Macdonald

CONTENTS

Winner

115 **A C Clarke**
Irish Giant
Seals
Devoted

Highly Commended

1 **Gill McEvoy**
The Plucking Shed
Water Lilies
Deer Signs

4 **Kristina Close**
Passport
The Lie
Indentations in the narrative

7 **Pat Borthwick**
In Praise of Grey
Beech House
Open Night at The
Observatory

Commended

13 **Colin Archer**
Coupled
Another Labour

15 **Norman Bissett**
In the Gorbals

17 **Josephine Brogan**
Trust Matisse

18 **George Carle**
All America's Dream

19 **Liz Cashdan**
Swimming Pools

20 **Derek Collins**
June 1944
Eva

22 **Ann Constable**
Ken

23 **Rose Cook**
The Everyday Adventures
of a Family Subject to
Hormonal Fluctuation

24 **Angela Cooke**
Outside People

25 **John Crick**
Camping in Wharfedale

26 **Clare Crossman**
Neighbour

27 **Judith Dimond**
Cuban Crisis

28	**Brian Docherty** Buggin's Turn	47	**Pauline Hawkesworth** The Sisterhood
29	**David Duncombe** Tongues	48	**Don Henderson** Nichols
31	**Margaret Eddershaw** Bosom Friends	49	**Doreen Hinchliffe** Elegy Remembering My Birthday
33	**Penny Feinstein** The Pond	51	**Jackie Hinden** Night Light
35	**Beryl Fenton** Urban Street Modern Art	52	**Mary Hodgson** Art Nouveau
36	**Sylvia Forrest** Portuguese Wall Hanging 17c Connections	53	**Marianne Hellwig John** In-between times
39	**Alan Franks** The Delivery of Spring	55	**Ursula Kiernan** Better than Night Nurse
40	**Berta Freistadt** Imitation of Walking	56	**Wendy Klein** Advice to Suicidal Poets
41	**Ann Gibson** School Run	58	**Bernard Landreth** Black Redstart
43	**R. J. Hansford** Casting Shed Word-Hoard	59	**Gill Learner** Neverland
45	**Chris Hardy** The Bombing Map	59	**Margaret Lewis** Elasticity Reliquaries

62	**Asit Maitra** Fullwallas	77	**Wendy Searle** Boy's Own
63	**Etelka Marcel** A.D. 2005: In Baghdad's Shi'ite District	78	**Gordon Simms** Kingston Bridge from Anderston
64	**Gol McAdam** Childhood Haven	79	**K. V. Skene** As Marsaxlokk Simmers
65	**Kathleen McKay** Stellar Maris	80	**Geraldine Messenbird Smith** The Magic Flute - Auditions
66	**C. E. G. Manwell** The Teddy Bear Game Kingfisher at Li Rangu	83	One foot in the Gutter **Lesley Mary Smith** I Collect Your Letter at the
68	**Walter Nash** Entre chien et loup	84	Stage Door **Michael Swan**
69	**Shirley Percy** Miss Armitage		A Blackbird Hopping Somewhere on a Small Yacht
71	**Michael Pooley** Waking	86	**Elizabeth Tate** Dahlias
72	**Diana Moen Pritchard** Facing South	87	**Maggie Tate** Joy Rider
73	**John Quicke** Prison Visitor	88	**Ruth Terrington** The Bird-bit
74	**Rod Riesco** The Slide	89	**Pam Thompson** Animadversions
75	**Andrew Murray Scott** A Bar on the Beach		Hoodie Season

92 **Harriet Torr**
    Hospital Room
    Death of a High-Riser

94 **James Turner**
    When Buildings Collapse

95 **Jenny J. Vuglar**
    In Time

96 **Joan Waddleton**
    The Piano

97 **Eddie Wainwright**
    Tatiana to Eugene:

99 **Huw Watkins**
    At Combwich

100 **Jean Watkins**
    Sheets
    Uffington

102 **Lyn White**
    Philosophy and Buoyancy

103 **Hamish Whyte**
    Her Laugh

104 **Sheila Wild**
    Byrd: antiphon for
        four voices

105 **Margaret Wilmot**
    Six Things My Father
        Told Me

106 **Linda Wilson**
    Someone, Somewhere

107 **Robin Lindsay Wilson**
    Soul Mates

109 **Janet Wiltshire**
    Nothing is Happening
    Owl

111 **Sue Wood**
    Esther

112 **Jan Woodling**
    Between Woking and
        Guildford
    All Hallow's Eve

114 **William Wood**
    Edouard Vuillard

119 **Biographies**

Gill McEvoy

The Plucking Shed

As we pluck, the air fills with a flour
of feather and dust: everyone sneezes.
The floor is pillowed in down and quill;
our footsteps smother in their folds of snow.

The plucking goes on and what you are
beneath your plumage reveals itself:
enormous prickly pears,
feather-pores like craters in your skin.

On the floor your other selves, the white plumed
creatures that we knew as geese, grow light and tall:
each time the door is opened soundless skeins
of ghosts rise up, thread their way
into the blanket of the night.

Water Lilies

Tonight I'm stepping out of this old skin:
watch it swirl away into the drain
vanishing in suds and foam.
All those years of making, and it didn't suit.
No time now to waste.

I wrap my raw self in a wreath of towel,
paddle to the wardrobe in wet feet.
In my wake a burst of strange,
dark water lilies bloom.

Deer Signs.

We're following a blue tourist bus
that ricochets off potholes, explodes into sky,
showering our windscreen in dust and grit.

Its driver is furious because he
'weren't contracted to have no car followin'.
So here we are, struggling to keep up

while he roars down America's dirt-roads,
shaking his passengers up like milk
and not giving a holy damn.

At last he loses us, his dust-cloud vanishes.
Now I must read the map. Except,
out here in the Badlands, there are no signs.

We stop. Just ahead of us there is a deer, humped
on the thin grass verge, its pale tan sides still new,
and I know we're hot on the trail.

Later I'll check the wheels of that bus for blood:
out here in the Badlands things are still bad enough.

Kristina Close

Passport

You sigh, pack your hair
and eyes into a new photo,
into this license to climb map lines between cliffs,
between sheets of straits
flap flapping like wet linen
on corrugated iron ports.

Getting away – a limited phrase
with no object.

The plane trails again and like Rapunzel,
each new sea opens its seaweed arms

and your languid sigh
cools my hair with your breath,
cools the air that dives into far-below caves,
their doors shut at high tide.

Dear diary,
today we reached Monterey.
I am standing on the balcony of the lilac room
in the travel brochure
and I am not happy.
The swallows are fishing the sky
above the bay,
still

a cliff is a cliff.
Venus has dropped her arms
in the sea and is crying.

The Lie

His face turns to her
smooth, as liquidly calm
as the passing
foot outside the basement window
that is lifting, rising over a sprung
crack in the pavement.

Indentations in the narrative

My feet are too light on this stone.
It is as if there is no one here.

I wake in the morning dry.
My mouth is dry. The light is dry.
The bees are living in reeds.

The well has forgotten his duty.
Already there is a bird nesting in the cool
darkness. I can hear its small satisfactions
in the bite of the day.

Do you want me to wait. Do you want me to stare
into the sun until I am blind.

Pat Borthwick

In Praise of Grey

Of all colours
grey paints the wisest.
It tiptoes along the rosary
to illuminate uncertainties.
Its muscley arms brace apart
basalt and marble pillars.
It can upturn chiaroscuro's hat
brimful with expectation.
Shadows try and hide in it
and fail, grey's finger
pointing to the temporary
moon and sun.
Grey patrols the edges
and folds between oil and salt,
between falling snow
and fallout's blot.
In the kiln
it sits astride the pyrometer
soaked equally by
the white heat of porcelain
and cold, empty shelves.
It links albatross and water boatman,
panther and cabbage white.
Grey is the colour
of our ganglions and brain cells.
It is fired with endless desire
for all things to be possible.
And this, in lakefuls,
I leave to you my son,
and for you, his sister,

knowing how
he'll share all this with you,
a silver paddle
to keep it stirred and fresh.

Beech House

The older folk keep to their beds,
their wings tied with muslin.
Through his netted window
my uncle is content to see the moon
open its bright eye. Or is it the sun?
A single snowflake?
Strange, how the snow is so accurate.
Year by year, in a sort of symmetry,
it finds and fills his window, only his,
whichever street he's living in.
His grandchildren's children
have built snowmen in the garden
like last month's, and down the corridor
where wheelchairs and zimmers
are parked for the night.
Some have been abandoned,
their owners gone missing.
They'll not get away with it.
Up on the poop deck,
a row of uniforms with telescopes.
They'll sort it out. On his single shelf
there's a biscuit and a meteorite.
And a ship in a bottle painted with stars.
In the bedside drawer, he keeps the Queen
and his medal. And his house keys because
he's *not staying long. Go away,* he shouts,
as they try to untie his bib, *Go away.*
All hands. Up hammocks. Bring my quadrant.
Dead reckoning time. He's bent at the window.
Newton, Copernicus, Einstein, Herschel,
Aristoteles, Hercules, Julius Caesar,
Billy, Hell, Beer, Parrot, Short, Airy. There!

That's where we landed, he says, pointing
to the moon, the sun, a snowflake,
still naming craters. *Such magnificent desolation.*
Outside, the beech trees applaud fidgety stars
and the man at the window counting.
Do you know our module has only one ascent engine?
There is never a second chance.

Open Night at the observatory

SATURDAY, SEPTEMBER 21st
The Museum Gardens
7pm

The sky is smart and polished.
I'm in the queue, eager to reach Saturn.
   There's more in my pockets than I'd known:
scarab beads, a Feng Shui pen, a loop of string,
De'Anna's '100 Magic Prayers', Old Moore's, an
unwrapped chew, a plaster and something sharp
until at last, I'm through the door
and can see a spiral stair
that will lead me round and up
through the ticking of time clocks, past
the long pendulum and astral charts,
past mahogany and brasswork
to an octagonal platform
with the 4½" refractor
tilted and extended through the dome
out towards Saturn.
   You, with your Snoopy watch,
are talking numbers
with necklaces of noughts
and now have your fingers over mine
over this knurled wheel,
bringing Saturn into focus
as clear as that cup and saucer
spinning from my mother's hand
the day I told her there was no God.
   You show me how to cup my hands
near the eyepiece and, on a cone of light
float this planet in them,
this planet, a billion miles away
and as close as you behind me now,
your breath melting its magnetic ice
and mine.

    Saturn's rings cast tight shadows
as does your single one, its gold
multiplying down the scope
towards a far off single point.
    I rewind home
a long way beyond zero,
knowing I must return you to her,
my hands deep in my pockets,
that wretched rabbit's foot
I should have thrown out long ago,
    Saturn still up there
spinning at an impossible angle
while I'm about to find
the numbers you wrote
on the crumpled bit of paper
    I'm fingering
near this sticky sweet.

Colin Archer

Coupled

The tattooed lady on his upper arm
Is ageing too; her skin once smooth and lusty pink
Has wrinkled now, as grey as his. Her mighty breasts
Pointedly thrust towards some lurid heaven
Have drooped towards his scrawny elbow;
Pudenda willing in transparent veils
Have vanished now inside a crease of flesh.
He tries to flex his muscles: she'll no longer dance.

They've been together sixty years, and she alone
Has never left him. Inseparable at the end
They had not planned to age and fade together.
He seldom stops to look at her these days
Except on lonely nights through thick-lensed tints.
Still, they share a bed and maybe even now
He dreams of lust. And she – who knows? –
Of grandchildren? Cups of tea? Or decent clothes?

Another Labour

Every month I am up this ladder
Trimming back the ancient creeper
Which softens the harsh outlines of the house
But threatens to strangle it.

Already it has half-covered upstairs windows
Ready to steal another Summer's light,
And soon its tentacles could claw at the door
And trap us inside for ever.

At my age, they say, I should get a 'little man',
But thirty feet up I *am* that little man
Still tackling a Herculean task, a Hydra
Which grows ten heads for every one I slash off,

and labouring with lofty thoughts,
I could easily slice through the telephone wire
Hidden in all the thrusting new growth
And get cut off from family, friends, all I love.

Norman Bissett

In the Gorbals

Twa Glesca keelies,
wee Fenian guttersnipes,
bricht-eyed ragamuffins,

tufted like waxwings,
inner-city sparras
wi' tackey bits

an' corrugatit socks
aroon their ankles,
Bert Hardy bairns

trailin' through canyons
o' grubby tenements,
dubs, dog shit,

Joan Eardley weans,
wi' cauliflower ears
an' latent strabismus,

aff-white knees,
breid-knife haircuts
an' snottery ganseys

clutchin' their bag,
their precious bawbees
an' each ither

by the haun,
head off chirpily
fir mammy's messages,

milk, Mirror, Woodbines,
keechie wee rapscallions,
stampin' the sivers,

like fallen angels
meanderin' towards heaven
intae the licht.

Josephine Brogan

Trust Matisse

Banality's the spur: his wife brings home
four goldfish in a jar and soon
he finds the exact bowl to set them in
a leafy plumped-up corner. Now comes
the real conundrum. Mine, nights when I was younger
I'd gaze on – fine straight lines in the water,
goggle eyes height of the table – so I'd learn
the memory-span, the point the horizon began
and ended, whereas for him the moment seen
is absolute, it glistens. Think of the chromatic
balance: jump-suit orange, fantastic
spiky green. A water-pasture. Creatures humble,
indefatigable. Drawing me into little
humdrum lives, and him straightway into Fame

George Carle

All America's Dream

The cool cusps of ice
hid in the fridge
waiting to be twisted
from the plastic tray
and manhandled
clinking into the glass

the fat man
squeezed a cut lemon
and teased the ice

he salivated as
all America's dream
frothed and spilled
over Betty's nice counter top

by the fridge he saw
four bottles of beer
and recalled his father's breath
as he was beaten
and promised not to tell.

Liz Cashdan

Swimming Pools

How strange that summer's underwater glide
when the splash-muffled air raid siren pulled
us up short and, feet touching bottom, we stood
shoulder-deep at the shallow end; we stared up
eyes screwed against sun, saw tiny planes
scratching the sky, marked at least in memory
by black swastikas. Then a cry from mother,
and fumbling the ladder, we scrambled out,
dived for the shelter of the brick-built lavatories.
The whine of the planes faded towards Coventry.

I don't remember the colour of my swim suit,
but the body-twitch shiver, and the trickle of
water down my legs are swimming pool dreams.
Today as I climb out of this sunlit pool
in Constantia a motorbike roars uphill under
Table Mountain, unsettling the garden quiet.
I grab a towel, slip wet-foot indoors,
drying the drops of water off my skin.

Derek Collins

June 1944

Black lines on newspaper maps
show the Allied fronts advance.
On the radio John Snagge announces
the Allies land in Normandy,
Rome's liberated. (Dad's somewhere there.
His last letter wished he could exchange
Italy and Rome for England and home.)
At the Classic newsreel bombs
parabola down in periodic sequence.
White puffs appear on grey earth.

In school we save paper, draw
narrow margins in our exercise books,
reach the Romans in history.
English literature at the Odeon,
Laurence Olivier on a white charger
wins Agincourt in Technicolor.

The tram is full this morning.
We chatter, swop cigarette cards
of football heroes,
alight, turn right for school,
maroon blazers bearing the school motto,
"Toil no soil."

"Arbeit macht frei."
Train doors slide open,
suitcases, bundles, thrown out.
Boys gulp air,
are ordered to the left.
A girl follows, tries not
to dirty her gold shoes.

Eva

The Intercities speed by the hospital,
slice each day in regular routine,
but she doesn't hear them as, alone,
she runs down Bottle Bank by Pipewellgate

to Haggie's Rope Works with her father's bait.
Returns to the present's moment by moment
as she strains to place me,
my photograph on her bedside table.

"Willie's son?" "Yes, you remember,
when I was small, you'd take me
to Saltwell Park to feed the ducks,
hold my hand as I paddled at Whitley Bay."

I offer her the memories she once gave me.
Now they melt away as her snowcake did on my tongue.
"Willie's son. You'll know George then.
He hasn't been for a while."

The Intercity carries me from her bed,
brings me back to stand at her grave
among the funeral commonplaces for the very old.
"No sort of life." "She was waiting to die."

In the empty kitchen I catch our laughter,
as canty by the fire in her chair
she tells me stories of the hostels
where she cooked, never waiting to live.

Ann Constable

Ken

Under the wide white sky,
dry fields pant,
and marching pylons threaten aridity
as the dust whirls in a little wind
among the old caravans, tin sheds, and piles of brick,
and over the baking concrete.

Two dry dogs roam, suspicious –
another at the end of a long chain,
rattles, scratching.

Ken walks out of the shadows,
staring at us through thick glasses,
and
from under his black thatch of hair,
smiles,
a slow stubbly grin . . .

Sweat stains his grey vest,
the only trace of moisture
in his dried up world.

Rose Cook
**The Everyday Adventures of a Family
Subject to Hormonal Fluctuation**

It is autumn. Through leaf tossed streets
a son rides his father's bicycle,
struggles to keep a balance.
In his room hangs the skeleton he made,
festooning a surfboard,
backdrop to a young life
while in the kitchen is his mother,
labile as a Guy Fawkes sky,
cursing the demented milkman,
who leaves her daily supply of hormones,
sometimes one or three, nine or none,
there is no pattern or sense to it,
every day a surprise.

But who is in charge of the milkman,
you want to ask her, but she may kill you,
because he left seven bottles today and she drank them all.
Instead she leaves a note: *Have gone to Uruguay
for a while, until the snows are gone. Suggest
lasagne tonight. Have a nice Christmas.*
Her husband sighs and puts the kettle on.

Angela Cooke

Outside People

We sit about or go tentative walks to the W.C.
We do not read. There's too much going on
and always noise.
The trolley comes. We panic if we miss it.
It is the centre of the day – and the meals
which lie stiffly on the plates, each portion
too neat, like dolls-house food – no gravy.

Half the ward is glass. Cheaper than real walls.
The windows weary us. There's nothing to see
but sky without cloud and too much sun.
We have no protection, only our beds.
We are surprised at the hours we fritter away in sleep.

The visitors come with their outside faces.
They sweat in their outside clothes. They bustle in
with anxious smiles, bracing themselves
hoping they're ready for whatever we, the ill
might throw at them.

We are like war veterans who talk of things
never to be shared with those who drop in
with flowers, who busy themselves with that other world
and are convinced they will live for ever.

John Crick

Camping in Wharfedale

Morning licks the tent's
blue canvas yellow. From my bed
a triangle frames a poached-egg sun,
a rubik cube of crops,
a road up which a postal van
climbs like a thermometer reading.
The land lays out its jumpsuit.
I stretch all ways, and the day fits.

    On the sky's page,
    a cow felt-tips
    a thick brown O of sound;
    paranoic cocks
    drill and steeple echoes
    down the dale;
    a child's crying
    clobbers my ears.

Cows, cocks, child – fanfare
and noises off . . . and I,
woken to a strange place,
a hill massaged by light,
see you return across the field.
At your feet a breeze prints
heartlines on the grass.
I will touch you. I am home.

Clare Crossman

Neighbour

One of my friends' mother had a house like this.
Draughty, with picture windows, you could feel the weather
even when the doors were closed. Visitors would arrive
                                                    unannounced,
sit up late at night in the kitchen's coffee smell or sleep
in the attic filled with bags and trunks amongst the dust
and sand of Spain, where she travelled every year.

This corridor is full of hats and shoes. Vases and jugs,
the deep earth-coloured ochre pots she has made for 30 years.
Bare boards and white walls contain the sun. Each room
a cracked canvas that has caught somewhere remembered.
Whenever I am here I feel an easing, as if nothing
is irrevocable and I could begin again.

I walk out and find her in a too large overcoat, digging in the
                                                            garden.
'It's the texture of things that's important,' she says.
'Not many really see that.' We exchange firewood and books,
and sometimes talk together. When she's not absent following
the light along the coast, or bashing out clay, refusing
to compromise concerning the details of sunshine and shadow.

Judith Dimond

Cuban Crisis

Framed by the window, a sleek cat stands
parked like a Cadillac on scruffy grass
and glares at a plump pigeon
whose feathers ruffle in the wind.

The strutting bird displays no fear –
stares back in fact with equal disdain.
Both dare the other to invade
their unmarked territory,

neither party aware of me
hands sudded at the sink.
Each holds its breath and so do I
until lids blink simultaneously.

They wheel away, the cat
swallowed by the hedge
the pigeon steering to the eastern sky
and I breathe easy again.

Brian Docherty

Buggin's Turn

There's nothing wrong with job rotation
provided someone will train or mentor you.
But if you're simply handed the cook's apron
& chequered pants, given a knife, a large pot
and a barrowload of dead mammals, birds
& vegetables the likes of which you've never
seen before, then told there are 60 tired, dirty,
& hungry cons, you have to pray to whichever
deity you imagine might be on prayer duty
today and might actually care what happens
to the people PanGal dumped here forever,
and hope you do a better job than John 6,
Tom 4 and Melvin 2, who either couldn't cook
at all, poisoned two whole tables at lunchtime
or got bitten by something that wasn't quite dead.
Death is the only cure for septicaemia here.
Already I have taken too long to skin & gut
the animals, gotten a rash from the veggies,
lost the salt and spilled one tub of water.
The sundial says I have 15 minutes to provide
a hot nourishing meal for men fingering weapons,
questioning my family & doubting my prospects
of a happy & virtuous life beyond sundown.
If there were anywhere to escape to & survive,
any chance of stumbling upon a lost spaceship
buried in the sand, or friendly natives to shelter
me and make me an honorary clan member,
I'd wad up my apron, toss it in the fire
and try to think of a suitable Oscar Wilde
or Groucho Marx quote as my exit line.

David Duncombe

Tongues

Your limousine transfer. The deep voice
plucked us from the wheelie suitcase trundle
of Kennedy's arrivals, reassured us
with the sound of our own names. Uniformed, big,
Afro-American, he talked us past
the line of ticking yellow cabs. You need
to watch these guys, they sometimes lose their way,
they only just arrived themselves. Russians,
Albanians, Koreans, Pakistanis,
and so on and so forth. Staring ahead
the drivers waited, not all-American yet.

He could tell we were Brits, so quiet, he boomed,
compared us with Japanese, Italians,
Germans, French . . . you name them, New Yorkers all
for the price of an airline ticket. Let's go.

The Lincoln's leather seats spoke comfort,
the radio's gospel music promised joy.
He sang in a choir, church every Sunday,
surprised we didn't, English and all that.
He liked roast beef, savoured the words. We searched
the Manhattan skyline, the gap telling more
than the Chrysler, bridges, the Empire State.
He delivered us to the 30/30,
wished us a wonderful week and meant it.
We nodded thanks, polite, he expected it.
An obese woman in a stinking fur coat
told us to get the fuck out of her way.

We slipped into the city like new sorts
of coffee bean into Starbucks, people
ready to try us out. They pronounced with care,
wanting us to take the right direction.

Our yellow cab, from Bleecker Street, stopped
and started as feathered divas blew kisses
from the gay procession for Halloween.
Our driver, Puerto Rican, hands off the wheel,
waved back, can you believe these guys? Himself
he believed in live, let live, America,
the power of language, the church, a happy home.
Wife no Spanish, mother in the same house
no American, so no arguments.
He interprets what they want to hear.
I guess the tip – we speak the same language.

Margaret Eddershaw

Bosom Friends

From Saigon's bright bustling
into the dark, cramped shop,
Aladdin's cave,
shelves of silk in strata
of sapphire, emerald, ruby.

She flows soft rivers
through her arms,
across the rush-matted floor,
over my shoulders,
hands dancing,
then framing me
with chosen fabric.

Sweat pearls form on her brow,
jet eyes twinkle beside
an ebony fall of hair.
A bonsai tree woman,
twiglike arms,
tiny trunk, swaying
in an imperceptible breeze,
slim legs,
two light, downward strokes
of a calligrapher's brush.
I dwarf her.

She clambers onto a stool
to measure my back,
calling figures to an assistant.
Cool hands turn me round,
pass the tape behind me,

across my bust.
She looks at the number,
hesitates, checks.
Our eyes meet.
Words rustling like leaves,
she says, 'Nice big titties!'
cups them in miniature fingers.
'I'd rather be *your* size,' I answer.
Women of the world, we laugh,
hug each other.

Penny Feinstein

The Pond

Yesterday with pitchfork, handsaw,
wheelbarrow and gumboots
I sorted out the pond.

I like to sit beside this pond,
no bigger than the kitchen table,
absorbed in the otherness of water life,
the unvoiced sounds, the timescale:
how frogs can be so motionless and sudden,
how larvae climb the iris leaves at day-break,
exchanging water for the sun,
and take until midday to emerge
as elegant, green-black dragonflies.

I have seen newt and bladder snail
lash and writhe in day-long battles,
the water round them juddering
with minute shock waves; watched
the balletic opening of water lily buds
and on sleepless summer nights heard
muted lapping among the reeds
as things shift and settle
beneath the rippled moon.

But . . . blanket weed has taken over,
hogging the light. Rushes crowd and jostle,
and the newts have left.
I wrestle with the waterlogged rootmass,
saw it into manageable chunks –
khaki convulsions in the water.
I hold my breath against the mud-stink,

plip back stranded snails and heave
the sodden gobbets into the barrow.

Today the pond looks clear but chastened.
A toad, crowned lopsidedly with duckweed,
lords it on a lily pad.

Beryl Fenton

Urban Street Modern Art

There's a Ben Nicholson on pavement
rectangles – a haphazard pattern
of small grey circles;
flat chewed gum.

There's a Jackson Pollock at the tree's
base, where roots have cracked
the asphalt and where a dog
peed, saturating and staining
those crevices.

There's an Anthony Caro against
iron railings where detritus
of a pedal cycle is
abandoned.

There's a Kurt Schwitters collage –
a palimpsest of torn posters
pasted in layers.

There's a Cristo wrapped around
bare tree branches, white plastic
bags, which wave like
happy ghosts.

There's all this to view, free.

Sylvia Forrest

Portuguese Wall Hanging 17c

This pale green silk will be a background
for summer afternoon dragonflies
flitting among reeds and water.

My husband inserts two proud cockerels, symbol of his house;
then adds his long-bodied dogs leaping with joy.
Two matching dragonflies are allowed on the edge of his design.

I stitch his latticed black circle,
outline his tentacle leaves,
fill a matched pair with small mourning-crosses.

And another week and another week passes.
He hangs my work in a high dark room.
I open the shutters and my dragonflies gleam.

Connections
Howick Northumberland
16th July 2004

This is the stuff that dreams are made of.
This rare fine day, this soft warm air.
The vast calm sea.
A far cry from last night's television:
That BNP member boasted how he'd beaten up a Pakistani.
Another said 'If they don't learn our language they can f..k off.'

This easy clay path is a donkey brown ribbon
and it keeps away from the edge of the cliff.
Earlier, our picnic rug had almost touched the drop.
I'd wanted to jump off, jump off,
but got stuck into homemade pizza.
Red wine lessened the tension.

A bus had arrived near our picnic spot.
Chattering children became a shifting line along the clifftop.
The cliff is a disorder of jagged outcrops.
The distant calm of low flat rock…
The height of Cullernose Point…
Tapering Cullernose is a collie's nose pushing into the sea.

I'd glanced to my right.
Durer's grasses, etched against the sky.
Nuremburg: his house closing as we'd reached it; we'd come back.
But pop music murdered sleep. Next morning I'd pulled out
                                             tent pegs,
while Mercedes, Audis and BMW's practising at the stadium,
sounded like that swarm of wasps above the restaurant's
                                             umbrellas in Weil.

We continue along the path where this poem began
and pass through a slit between blackthorn.

The Point's grassy top has patches of blue and yellow.
A cushion of sea-pinks clings to the edge.
We retrace our steps and go on to Howick Hall Garden.
Its charms take charge of time.

Hay is being cut in the daffodil meadow.
We wander through the Silver Wedding wood;
drink Earl Grey tea near the bronze of a skating pair.
Days pass.
In drenched Newcastle,
Earl Grey of Howick looks lonely on his monument.

Earl Grey, 'Friend of the People', instigator of the Reform Bill

Alan Franks

The Delivery of Spring

Now that the iron-bound winters have gone the way
Of high-rise blocks of flats and slam-door trains
And dog mess turning white on summer kerbs,
The spring comes in with a minimum of fuss
Like a pleasant-smelling woman returning from
The cloakroom to a conversation which
Was managing well enough while she was gone.

I never wanted to earn love over-easily,
Never expected to wake one significant morning
And note its delivery along with the rest of the mail;
Always rather believed that the genuine thing
Would come at the end of a coldness patiently borne
And cause in the ground a visible shift, and even
Sound like the clink of a key in the lock of the land.

Berta Freistadt

Imitation of Walking

Sometimes the pavement is
soft beneath my feet
pillows
sometimes mountains

one foot in front of the other
pick your feet up she used to say
it's no longer there unless
I follow in the slipstream
of a real walker
finding another's rhythm
some too tiring
sometimes someone
with a joyous swing

reminds me and I'm unknowable
unknown
heel down
knee up
who cut the strings
step plié step plié
I used to be a dancer

Ann Gibson

School Run

Big school is different.
No chatting at the gates
with other mums,
no hugs or open arms,
just sitting in the car,
waiting.

Has she seen me? Who's to know?
No wave of recognition,
no acknowledgement allowed
on either side.
I mustn't move a muscle,
only wait.

I watch her catwalk
straight towards the car,
no glance to right or left,
no friendly smile.
All sulky independence,
teenage angst.

The temptation,
to play old music loud
through open windows,
rev the engine, flash the lights
and hear her martyred whimper
"Muuuuum".

Or, stand beside the car,
shout a greeting,
wave and blow a kiss,

toot the horn.
That's all it would take to make her
catch the bus.

R. J. Hansford

Casting Shed

Moulds numb fingertips,
it's too cold to mix
but we can still strip-out.

Breaking an icy crust,
we tap the white shapes
from their bevelled trays.

We pit the body's heat
against a frozen universe;
our gloves are warming up.

Word-Hoard

Old English, Old Saxon,
Old High German, Old Norse,
Old Dutch, Old Frisian, sea-raider tongues;
they huddle together against the North wind.

Chewy as whale-meat,
they leave a tang of salt in our mouths;
grasping an oar, wielding a two-headed axe,
holding my ground in the shieldwall,
I swear by them, word-kinned.

Chris Hardy

The Bombing Map

There is a map which shows
where every bomb that fell on London
landed.
I did not believe this could be done
even when I saw it
but the hoardings
that once stood where a quartet fell
on the Lavender Hill junction
with the Wandsworth road
are on the map.

They used to fill these gaps with adverts
and petrol stations are a sure sign
of a hit.
This area has come up since those nights
when the Germans
veering left above the power station
dumped bombs they'd failed to scatter
on the docks
two minutes over London
lit up like a snake along its river.

There's a bathroom emporium now
where the blast took out
several triple-decker Victorians
down to the basement.
It recommends we soak
in a deep and gleaming bath
shaped like the tub of Telemakhos
the first thing they found at Pylos
another city burnt from roof to ground

by enemies we've forgotten how to fear.

And this reminds me of my mother's friend
a little more than friend I gather, once
who came back to his house
stuck in the side of a valley
with the sea in a wood below
came back from the emaciated edge
four years in a Japanese prison camp
and said thank God and America
and everyone
for the atom bomb.

Pauline Hawkesworth

The Sisterhood

The wedding gift –
a metal horse,
heavy, angular.
A weapon, she said;
use it once only
as one strike
is all you need
to stop an enemy.

When the burglar comes,
or the rapist, or vandal
hammers at your door,
press the cold back
of the horse into your palm
leaving its jagged hooves
free to flay-out.

Use all the non-horse power
folded by centuries of women,
secreted inside your wild forearm;
the one that will shield
your babies, protect them
within a hook of silken skin;
and release your power.

Don Henderson

Nichols

Nichols is white, polite and English, with a complexion pale from endless hours spent indoors at the piano, perfecting a talent for performing the music of fallen heroes from the past, kings of the keyboard like James P. Johnson, Jelly Roll and Fats. That's the art of his re-creation with his improvisation, lowdown delta sound of New Orleans, hot-style from Chicago and New York, a spicy mix like red beans and rice, with a delicate salad to follow; ragtime, honky-tonk, jazz-time, Harlem stride he's master of them all. His stubby strutting fingers striking at keys, punching out crisp redhot bundles of notes at tremendous tempo – rich musical tender. Then he's into a gentler mood, bringing us a ballad or the blues, a love song or a sad song to maybe streak our perspiring faces with a tear or two, before he bounces back just like Fats with his irrepressible humour. For an encore he leaves the stool, takes a soprano saxophone, shifts gear on the ensemble swing, lifts us up to higher ground with that Heavenly Music! Oh! Mr Nichols!

Doreen Hinchliffe

Elegy

Stripped bare of blossom by late April hail
your cherry tree stands naked in the park
lit by a watery sun that smears a trail
of pallid gold across its ancient bark.
Inside our room, a single washed out ray
uncovers dust around the barley twist
of your old chair. I brush it all away,
the dust you used to say I always missed.
Now, you are missed and what remains of you
remains beyond my reach, no matter how
I might imagine you in sunlight through
the window or along the cherry bough.
Our past, like blossom, can't survive the storm,
the sun is powerless to keep it warm.

Remembering My Birthday

Remembering my birthday is routine
you mark it with the same perfunctory kiss
while I am thinking of the might have been.

Each year your card swears love is evergreen
but cliché is a kind of cowardice
remembering my birthday is routine.

We sit in silence as the haute cuisine
is served. You try in vain to reminisce
while I am thinking of the might have been.

There's nothing we can do to change the scene
without a war there is no armistice
remembering my birthday is routine.

We stand on either side of our ravine
you wondering, maybe, how it came to this
while I am thinking of the might have been.

This ending isn't what we had foreseen
this slow descent into paralysis
remembering my birthday is routine
it's pointless thinking of the might have been.

Jackie Hinden

Night Light

All night the light winks on and off.
I watch its beam shine back
through the glass front door,
gilding the wall.

What is it wakes the light?
Crisp packet or paper cup,
predatory fox or cat?
Or the ghost of my son who always
slammed the gate?

Now no one comes except the paper or the post,
or the carer who cleans and shops
and calls me Kate although
my name is Catherine.

Mary Hodgson

Art Nouveau

(. . . as a decorative style it relied primarily on an organic and generative line . . . in which fundamentally unrelated images are often combined . . . seen for example in Mucha's posters. Enc. Brit.)

Standing on windy cliff I watched the kestrel
hovering apparently unconcerned, balancing
with ease against the air-stream, maintaining
stance, position – a ballet-dancer on points.
I could see the forward-curving head,
hooked beak; imagine eyes
beam-focussed downward, lasering
into scanty grass on the cliff face.

Suddenly, he stooped –
single black penstroke
etched on the air, gone in an instant,
flash of organic line,
fatal fusion of unrelated elements,
insubstantial Mucha poster, but
atavistic, existing from the start of time,
art non-nouveau.

Marianne Hellwig John

In-between times

When it's either too warm or too cool
and you don't know what to put on;

when they're either brilliant or sulky
and you don't know which way to turn;

when you're either running or falling
and unable to stay put;

when the other side's stonewalling
and you can't spin past the bat,

then it must be
autumn,
adolescence,
mid-life crisis,
cricket,
all the in-between times.

When the parsley's been sown and watered
and six weeks later there's still no sign;

when the golf-club, clock or handshake
reminds you there's another life to begin;

when there's lines of scribbles and deletions
and no completed shape in sight;

when there's inches of twisting roads on the map
and you're wondering where to stop for the night,

then it must be
spring,
retirement,
poetry,
travel,
all the in-between times.

Ursula Kiernan

Better than Night Nurse

There was a time I couldn't sleep. But now I have a lover
who's much better than Night Nurse or five million
silly sheep. It's good he hardly ever looks the same;
I like him in Ringmaster role with glitter eyes and whip.

I welcome his Marquis de Sade, though this may end
in pain. At times he will blow in as Peter Pan, but only
if I'm feeling Wendyish. Grimaldi knows which buttons
work for me; I like a tragi-comic vein. Quasimodo's cool.

Best of all, is his 'no prisoners taken' Ghengis Khan;
on the other hand, his Spooner is superb; all those –isms
send me straight to sleep. But if I'm still not Lethewards
inclined, then I'll settle for him in mud-wrestler role.

You ask, is this confusing? No, not really. I recognise
his vampire teeth. And then, he always smells the same;
of wheelie bins and dead decaying things. The bonus is,
I lubricate more freely when I'm almost dead with fright.

Wendy Klein

Advice to Suicidal Poets
for Anne Sexton

Do not
cradle a mug of cold beer
between your palms at 5 AM.
Sleep instead, with your back
against a low wall of dogs.

Take them everywhere.

With dogs at your heels
you won't stumble naked
from one dark room to another,
reassuring your still-good breasts
with hands that won't stop trembling.

Breathe in their pungent devotion.

Warm and insistent on
your restless ankles, it is
stronger than the sting of the
last chilled vodka
reminding your fingertips

you are not dead yet when you
reach the garage door, put your key
in the ignition. Stop before
the engine coughs, sighs, dies, and
listen for the sound of barking.

Get back indoors.

Face up to the challenge
of unconditional love.
You're saved, this time,
whether you like it or not.

Bernard Landreth

Black Redstart

I saw it – a slight black bird
with a red flash of tail –
on a roof in Navigation Street.

I was seventeen, waiting for a 41
in a queue of shop and office workers
which stretched beyond the shelter,
and I wanted to use my barely broken voice
to tell them: *Look up there!*
        A bird you may never see again.

But I was a novice in a world of adults
and only spoke in answers
so I didn't even tell
the tired-looking man beside me,
who I knew from the Treasurer's Department,
I just watched, surrounded and alone,
until it flew on to a chimney then away.

At home I ticked
my Field Guide to British and European Birds:
how could I know then
that as the book became unbound and feathered,
the memory would outlive the tick;
how could I know that I would still be able to see
the small rare bird,
as clearly as on that Birmingham rooftop,
when I was as old as the man who stood beside me –
whose name I have forgotten,
who may have died
having never seen a black redstart.

Gill Learner

Neverland

Remember the Odeon?
A liner docked in a suburban backwater, waiting
to carry us away. Wide steps to the great doors,
sticky sixpences to swap for other lives, the itch of plush
behind our knees. Saturday morning choruses
to the bobbing ball, adventures of flannel-shorted boys,
and girls in frocks with ribboned hair and Rinso'd socks,
who never had nits or sties, never swore, told lies,
and foiled the plots of men with shifty eyes.

Remember the Odeon?
How we watched the man on his Thursday ladder
slot new films into the display, craned to guess the letters
coming next. Megs went two nights a week to keep
her mother company while Dad was on the road.
Limited to matinées of Disney and Danny Kaye,
I nagged her for scraps: John Mills heroic in Antarctica;
Bogart swigging as he risked his boat;
Margaret Lockwood wicked with her beauty spot.

Remember the Odeon?
Tipsy on gaudy promises which began with a lion's roar,
a mountain ringed with stars, a turning world,
we plotted to leave on the Queen Elizabeth
showered with tears and flowers, set Hollywood ablaze.
I'd weave harmonies with Crosby while you'd share
step after firecracker step with Fred Astaire. But we'd be back
in frivolous hats, and furs that polished airline steps;
sign autographs and part our brilliant lips for magazines.

Then the doctrine of indulgences, differential calculus,
Arma virumque cano, and the periodic table intervened.

Margaret Lewis

Elasticity

A moment in Proust
Takes page after page to scan,
Let alone to write.
(What kind of pen
Did Proust have on his desk?)
Time, lost and sought and rediscovered
In another dimension,
Has to be so elastic!
Dante's downward view
Through the transparent spheres
Of the nine planets
And upward through the nine
Ecstatic orders
Is but a moment
In the search for the meaning
Of Beatrice's smile –
That mouth of all lost truth,
The science of the soul,
Whose griefs are felt
Even in Paradise.

Reliquaries

In centuries of filigree silverwork
Unbroken is the holy bones' repose.
The sacred text, buttressed by holy walls,
Dreams on, swooning with scent and song.
But the Holy Ghost slips out with the Sunday throng
And like a bee he plays with many a rose.

Asit Maitra

Fullwallas
(Flower Sellers)

Wearing a white dhoti
and a pair of sandals
he walks along the lane.
In his hands garlands
of marigold, sacred leaves.
He knocks at a few doors.
Sister, have a good Puja.
Housewives pay a Rupee
or two. On he goes again.
Dust scatters a spicy smell.
The tarmac melts in heat.
He trundles home and sits
on the floor to make garlands,
a prayer hums in his head.

Wearing stone-washed
jeans and Nike trainers
he chats to passers-by
that stop, choose and buy
roses, lilies well-wrapped
in plastic with price tags.
Fresh-cut flowers put a
smile on your lover's face.
Customers queue and laugh.
Cloud darkens the dusk.
He packs up his trailer,
hooks it to his blue Ford.
He whistles. The engine
sings all the way to home.

Fullwallas sell flowers, but they all sell a dream, a faith.

Etelka Marcel

A.D. 2005: In Baghdad's Shi'ite District

Dense clusters
of grey-green
conical caps –
with veils
the protective
layer –
bruised black
or blue
if handled
carelessly:
Brittle-gilled women
of the al-Mahdi
Army march
uprooted,
looking like
hand-picked mushrooms.

Gol McAdam

Childhood Haven
(1940s Style)

The thicket's track
The squat cottage

The bubbling paint
On the viridian door

The smell of candlelight
The glow of lavender bags

The love of a maiden aunt

Kathleen McKay

Stellar Maris

Mary's statue reaches arms across the harbour
where young boys dive into clear water
flecked with diesel drops. The ferry cuts through

The Narrows, lets its side down as it nears shore.
Cars start up. Two men in caps at the Cuan Arms
discuss Sean, who hasn't been over

for twenty years, but is just after getting back.
Hot whiskey slides down easy in November
when the sea mist rolls in and the long call

of the lifeboat breaks into your sleep. Inspectors
from England say the boat paint is toxic
to fish. Fungicides root, bed deep. This north

we're not without consequence. On clear nights
the Milky Way is visible, and a galaxy of stars;
Callisto and Cassiopeia, The Dog Star, The Plough

and at St Brigit's Well, rags on a hawthorn bush, alders,
scribbled wishes. *Please God cure her.*
Jesus grant my plea. In the cairns, boulders

cover stalagtites. Nitrates leach into the water
table. Fossils on the beach. On the shore
uprooted stones, people mumbling a prayer
say she went quick at the end, how people ought to.

C. E. G. Manwell

The Teddy Bear Game

In the basic form, they simply threw
your beloved teddy out of the window.
It proved you unpopular.

In the second version, they hid the bear
somewhere inside the dormitory.
The victim searched and begged, knowing
her bear could be lying down on the gravel.
If she found him, she won, but if
her nerve cracked and she told matron
she had emphatically lost.

Tracy claimed to be descended
from a knight who murdered Thomas à Becket.
They hung her teddy bear out of the window
on a gymslip girdle. One girl went down
to the loo on the landing, opened the window
and swung Eggle Bear like a pendulum.

I learned my lesson: to wear armour
protecting flesh from knives and needles.
I left Mr Pook at home.

Kingfisher at Li Rangu

From the namaliah, the netted bedroom,
we watched the dry land kingfisher
perched on a branch, diving for insects.
One morning, my father still in bed,
convalescent from malaria,
Saba, the head houseboy came in,
a bird in his hand instead of tea,
the fallen kingfisher.

That morning my lessons were by the bed
where my father lay, unshaven.
For art lesson, we all three drew
the kingfisher perching on our fingers.
We tried to feed it, it would not eat.
After three days it died.
My father skinned it and pinned
the skin to a board to dry in the sun.
Small black ants came and cleaned the skull.

Two years the skin was my favourite toy.
I stroked the feathers, comparing their silk
with the sharp strong isosceles beak.
In Juba it lay in my trunk of toys.
When we left, it remained in Africa.

Walter Nash

Entre chien et loup
(Twilight, 28°N 17°W)

Between a daylight and a dark,
between a visor and a veil,
evening begins;
so cool the air, so sweet,
jewels of lamplight glint between
the velvet pauses of the street –
diamond, amber, tourmaline,

and for an hour the world is held
floating upon a languid state
of timeless calm;
nothing will happen here
until a sea-breeze breaks the spell,
and music starts, and crowds appear
for shopping, strolling, dining well,

and so the neon signs will blaze
and fill the plaza with a crude
semblance of life,
a parody of light,
but at the edges of the town
true darkness brings the enormous night,
silent, mocking, glittering down.

Shirley Percy

Miss Armitage

In the beginning was Miss Armitage.
Recently arrived from Park Street Infants
we had minds without form and void
in need of her Religious and Moral Instruction
on Tuesday mornings. Straight as soldiers
in single file, we filled up
huge desks belonging to the top class.
Feet, not quite reaching the floor,
dared not fidget, for unlike our young Miss King,
Miss Armitage was very strict.
Solid, uncompromising, arms folded
she eyed us all for a fierce moment
of pre-creation silence. We sat
even stiffer, even stiller. Yet that
voice when it came, gruff, booming, was the
voice of an enchanter. Ancient words
echoing that chilly spring morning showed us
the spirit of God moving
on the face of the waters, making
a greater light, sun, and a lesser, moon.
Brief brightness haloed awe-struck heads
on the front row. Dianne did not sniff.
Sandra did not scratch. We swam
with the great sea monsters of the deep,
walked out with every creeping thing
on new made land, which put forth grass.
Within that plain Victorian classroom
God planted a garden, eastward, in Eden
where Adam and Eve walked, naked.
A pause. An explanation: 'naked' was
not her favourite word, to be reserved

at the present time for Bath Night, when
it might be next to godliness.
Adam and Eve disobeyed, ate the fruit
of the tree whereof they were not to eat.
Guiltily they hid. Miss Armitage
would soon have had the truth from Adam,
as did God. We thought him
a sneak to have blamed Eve. Next week
we would meet Noah, the One Righteous Man
and learn of the Great Flood. But for now
questions on Genesis one-to-three.
Having walked through a scary
vivid paradise, we answered well.
And Miss Armitage saw that it was good.

Michael Pooley

Waking

Often in the night I wake, to peer into the dark
cradle where you sleep. I cannot sleep for the need
to gaze at you, still enthralled by your arrival,
still wondering at your being here . . .

And each time I look, I am filled
with an elation, yet one which also frightens me –
as though even in the midst of joy I suddenly doubted
how I could hold and care for so much,

as though only now I began to comprehend
how fierce and how tender are my feelings for you,
how deep already your claims upon me,
what I must do, how I must be.

Diana Moen Pritchard

Facing South

Cloud hangs like a dull, grey curtain.
Its hem, a mist brushing a grey sea.
There is no fine line between them,
no obvious join, no horizon,
just a faded, lead-pencil rubbing;
sea distinguished only by minute
flauntings of white froth.
It's the first day of another year
of hope and love, yet fundamental fear.

John Quicke

Prison Visitor

A finger print captured for display
near a mug shot, name and info on a clipped
identity card, pockets emptied into orange
plastic trays for X-rays, keys and valuables
stowed away in a locker – after a sniffy look
and a touchy frisk, I enter the antechamber.

Frozen in a pose, amongst the mums and mates,
in a strong glass box with doors at either end,
I wait for a signal but only a routine rattle
of keys releases us from the strain of no eye contact,
and thoughts of surveillance in every crevice
up above.

Now in the bowels of the tomb, a white shirted
officer on a plinth allocates rooms, speaks
at me from a distance, like an old fashioned boss,
points me towards a no man's land of cubicles,
to the meet with a cleaned up prisoner who does
his best to work out who I am, and what

I'm up to with my line in cheery chat
and probing questions, a hopeful enterprise
to find the gold in what's been written off,
to steal it from under the noses of the guards
and those who put him here, plus selves
that prompted from within.

Others are trying to find the treasure too.
I watch them use their tools in practised ways
and cart their jewels of insights off in notes.

Rod Riesco

The Slide

We climbed the ringing treads
embossed with iron letters:
Wicksteed, Kettering.

The swoop of painted rails,
the grip and swing,
the letting go

that took you by surprise –
your thin spine in the blue dress,
two bunches in the breeze.

You shot down the brass tongue:
suddenly you were small,
elsewhere, transparent –

you never stopped,
across the darkening park
beyond the gathering of trees,

your tiny constellation,
gift of being
in trust to yearless years.

I wasn't prepared
- but neither were you –
not yet, not then.

I turned and placed my heels
on Wicksteed,
Kettering,
all the way
to the torn and tussocky ground.

Andrew Murray Scott

A Bar on the Beach
(Arenal D'en Castell, Menorca)

Under a canvas awning, Engelbert sings
to an empty bar and our wicker chairs
on duckboard, facing west,
clouds streaked –
a masterpiece of burning embers.

Early moonlight frosts
the rim of my glass, a laser
searching amber water
for late swimmers.

Stars emerge and torchlights
where couples stroll the sand.
The aroma of grilling meat trails
like music in the sooty air.

Everything is posed,
set in its true place,
between moon and sun.
Life pauses, richly ambivalent,
stilled, half-over, half-begun,
caught out being something else.
What was melancholy, out-of-focus,
now seems comedic, a farce –

Then the cocktail hour is over.
A night wind swings coloured lights,
karaoke noises Engelbert aside.
We stumble onto cool sand.

And see, from the cliff-top
our great fire, a single red coal,
lingering in the imagination,
long after it's gone out.

Wendy Searle

Boy's Own

He shoots through the stream, bucks then twists,
kicking up wheelies among the speeding cars
and wins startled hoots from motorists
who skid, squealing from his advances.

An OAP at the bus stop clutches her heart.
Two pedestrians freeze as the sleeping
zebra rears, then sprint across in alarm
with teeth flashing at their heels.

From grumbling, the vagrant changes gear
to rusty barks of laughter. On cue we do
as bid by this director of his own adventure,
too in shock to suggest a veto.

On and off the pavement he weaves
again, waves his bicycle like a cape
at the traffic's charges, avid to deal
direct with the beast and feel its shape,

jabs two fingers at a blaring near-miss,
wants it his, not like the screen's numbing
tease, but his skin plugged in, his
own soft network thrumming.

Gordon Simms

Kingston Bridge from Anderston

Tyres skim the motorway, stippling light
to prick out the tarmac's dirt-soaked skin,
oily seed that sharpens in the rain.
Glasgow glazes over. Inebriates, insomniacs
stare at windows, hear an early-morning train,
see pre-dawn streaks of red and white stretch
the viaduct to abstraction, a kinetic Jackson
Pollock splashed on charcoal grey. Above
the glow the sky holds back another day,
reflects the needlepoint of treads, then tracks
them in wide ripples through the night.
Snatched dreams spiral to some universe,
beyond the range of humdrum daily travel,
where motion's always smooth, direction right.

The soundless cars continue on their course.
But here each journey's made of sweat and fear:
corpuscles swerve and skid in sheets of spray.
Our progress is of fire, ash and rubble, spewed
gravel from some comet, extinct, anonymous.
The Clyde breathes fog. Street-lamps serve
as stars. I turn, reaching too late for sleep.

K. V. Skene

As Marsaxlokk Simmers

under a fat February sun
we hover over our second drink,
elbow the stained formica between us,
as sleepy as the moored *luzzu*
(even Osiris's eyes holiday on Holy Days)
bobbing and blinking at the tagalong children
tossing half their crisps to overfed ducks,
as limp as the wet nets drip-drying along the quay.

Only the Sunday market looks wide-awake
and a sudden in-your-face breeze
breaks the sound/scent barrier –
Madonna's heady hymn to herself
amid swordfish, squid, plaited strings of garlic,
olives, oranges, Gozo's *tal-bzar*,
just baked bread and litres of local wine.

Behind us,
brilliant yellow buses drive up,
                disgorge,
                    drive on –
as happiness usually does.

                luzzu – traditional Maltese fishing boats
                        with eyes painted on the prow
                tal-bzar – peppered goat's cheese

Geraldine Messenbird Smith

The Magic Flute – Auditions

The old gym smells of sweat
and plimsolls, at one end
by a stage of wooden blocks,
a strange man sits at the piano
reading a score.

Haulwen sits on a trestle table
swinging her feet in white socks
and sensible brown shoes.
Together we gaze in awe
at the newcomers,
real opera singers!

Marcus bounces about importantly,
good-humoured, but anxious.

Two younger boys hang,
upside down, from the wall bars,
demonstrating indifference.
Their ties, obliterating
mouths, noses, eyes,
make faces unrecognisable.

Sullen older girls whisper in groups
ignoring boys who interest them.
They buff their nails while they wait
and from the corners of their eyes
slyly examine the visiting tenors.

I examine Haulwen more closely.
Surely a dab of powder?

the faintest touch of lipstick?
and the scent of Evening in Paris?
I'm conscious of the age-gap.

One foot in the gutter

"One foot in the gutter."
That's what she used to say
about neighbours and others,
a term of abuse and scorn.
I didn't understand.

We'd sit on the kerb,
both feet in the gutter,
waiting patiently for passing cars,
writing registration numbers
In tiny red books with pencil stubs.
But she didn't mean that.

She said it about my Nana Peg.
Was it something to do with being Irish?
Did it mean me, part Irish?

At seventeen, walking home late,
my three inch heel snapped.
For a while I peg-legged along,
leaning on Eric,
but from Woolwich to Plumstead,
that's a very steep hill,
and it was hard going, until
I thought to walk, broken-shod foot
on the kerb, the other in the gutter.

Laughing and giggling our way home
from late-night dancing at the
Hot Club of London,
enjoying ourselves too much,
we were probably just what she meant.

Lesley Mary Smith

I Collect Your Letter at the Stage Door

He thinks too much, this character,
and I fall heartfully into him, stretching his arm,
or his foot as your unscented paper bends
thin in my pocket through three acts,
the sweat soaking it, my fingers touching it,
my voice – you do not trust it as much as you trust silence –
flaying line by line this man I might love
as if flesh, ruddy and sinuous, tied my hand to his.

Or this disrobing, where I abandon him
in exhausted unpeeling of my face
from his, the messages
he semaphores into the glass: Stay!
And I want to accede, lay my head, still wigged,
my neck, still itching from the rough seam on my taken-in costume,
on the chipped wood, among the rosettes
of tissue and crushed epidermis.

I unfurl your letter:
I line it up, creased, against the dressing room mirror.
It flutters in the draft from the door,
a faint pulse. You would recognise now
only my narrow iris, the dilated pupil.
You would say that was enough, burrow into me, looking
at my one still-made-up eye in the speckled glass,
fighting me to a stripped and desecrated skin.

Michael Swan

A Blackbird Hopping

From where they sit him
by the window
he can see a blackbird hopping,
each hop separate,
each hop a thing in itself,
each hop a whole story,
from beginning to end.
And the beak
yellow, shading a little,
a special yellow,
different from the walls,
or the doctor's notebook.
And the black wings –
so many blacks;
the nearer wing
reflecting more than the other,
perhaps,
as the bird turns a little.
At night
he lies awake
and sees the hops,
each hop separate,
each hop itself,
each hop a whole story.

Somewhere on a Small Yacht

In a moment of reduced attention
during the Gloria
I speculate about the bassoonist.
She looks like a lot of fun –
married, perhaps, to a stockbroker,
but open to alternative suggestions.

The bassoonist, meanwhile
with 84 bars to go
before her next entry
is considering the tenor.
He looks kind, prosperous, and unmarried.
She pictures a large house in Esher
where he lives
with his old mother.

The tenor, for his part,
while performing impeccably,
is a victim of churning fantasies
involving the black lady in the front row
her younger sister
and a small yacht on the Caribbean.

And somewhere
on a small yacht,
perhaps on this
but more probably on another planet,
the stockbroker,
the tenor's old mother,
and the black lady's sister
are playing five-card stud
with the composer.

Elizabeth Tate

Dahlias

they reminded me of sea urchins at first
or coral
marooned amongst the jumble.

red globes on stalks
alien plunder in a jam jar
bright wounds from the deep
each petal rolled
downwards.

dead man's fingers stiff
insistent not trembling as I'd imagined
the Emperor's chrysanthemums
in a border of Famille Rose.

Mexican apparently
more Mapplethorpe than natural
history cultivated by a student
of Linnaeus unequivocal and outrageous.

man-made these hybrids
a composite
designed to bloom when days are short.

and I returning from Eden
to this borrowed table
weary from too long in the sun
and wanting
to make the most of what is left
burn under their determined stare.

Maggie Tate

Joy Rider

I'm asleep when you enter,
your agile body squeezing
through a tight aperture.
I'm asleep as your hands grope,
asleep as fingers explore and evaluate.
I don't smell your sweat
as you falter and fumble in the dark;
I'm wrapped in dreams.

I awake to a trail of my clothes
discarded like frenzied sex.

For you, it was a quick in-and-out job,
climaxing early on finding the key.
Outside, you savoured the pleasure
as key slipped into lock,
ignition sparked first time.
Revving my Clio,
you drove away leaving
behind your calling card.

Ruth Terrington

The Bird-bit

Pastry's a knack that comes from making do
in the lean years. My mother had that deft
economy, seizing on every curl
from the pie's rim. She'd learned her thrift

right from a girl. (*Her* mother would slice ham
nearer the bone than Truth; would spread
butter like gold-leaf!) But after all was done
another imperative remained, unsaid:

from the floured board she'd pinch and pull
together the moist scraps, and shape
them into the rough knob she used to call
the Bird-bit. Solemnly we'd put it to bake

alongside the proper food. When it was done
we'd throw it, warm, onto the grass and watch
the starlings squabble over it. No-one
bothered to spell it out: simply, for each

harvest we knew some leeway must remain,
an untouched margin. This was the true
thrift, leaving a mite for those to glean
who in *your* want would do the same for you.

Pam Thompson

Animadversions

I give you the Black Bank pub: firkins stacked in a yard;
stale beer smell, rainwater overflow:
somebody's son, somebody's daughter, somebody's
. . . and this is morning: the kind of early
common to the 'seventies'. Sodium street light, yellow, dim.
You have been sitting on that felled tree between the lovers,
before the shot or shots, before no song, and no Corporation buses,
maroon and cream, nor Midland Reds which could be the name
of roses, brick red beauties, near the railway line, where,
in the summer of 1973, those shots failed to permeate
the miasma of cram, was it King John or the Gothics in triplicate?
For Mrs Macauley . . . The Crawl . . . but not Mrs Slinn
with bee-stung eyelids, nor Mr Palmer,
young endangered male with suntanned epiglottis
A whistle, shush of wheels: the coal train from Keresley.
And it's Latin, Mr Holland, apoplectic, aneuristic,
Salvete Puellae, trousers and jacket, matching shade of parchment
You never gave a thought to the boy from your class in junior school;
gapped teeth, too wide shorts. But you do now. Peering down
onto the road where the line was. Mystery of a word, *amputate.*
This morning, though, I give you a pale primrose light
like a promising sky behind white blinds on what was a bedroom
                      window.
You'll think of angel hair spun around an old-fashioned tree.
Early. A tree that once shed its needles. And it's nowhere near
                      Christmas.
This is the 'seventies'. Nor anything like home.

Hoodie Season

1. Shot

Everywhere, hoodies.
This was the season of the scare.

Cowled youths in shadows,
shot from below.

In a restricted space,
wouldn't you look dangerous
as the photographer closes in like a hunter?

2. Your new hoodie

Buying it, you were more concerned
about the spot on your lip;
kept glancing in shop mirrors,
fretted that it would put the girls off.

Then you dipped into your rolling
long armed, broad shouldered gait,
hormonal man-boy, *built*
but not as tall as some of your mates.

Will I get tall? I catch your smell.
Cheap hair gel, sweat, Lacoste,
bought duty free on a trip to Budapest
where there was no hoodie scare,

just the Danube looking famous,
statues of heroes in a public park,
and young people picking lilacs on Sunday,
to perfume their grandparents' houses.

3. Notice outside a shopping-mall

You are not allowed to enter with your hood in the up position

What might a boy in a hoodie do?
Slap you down? Kick you around?
Take a picture on his mobile phone
and send it round the school?

Or

(Hood in the down position)

Capsize a skateboard.
Smoke some weed in a cul-de-sac.
Litter that part of the road
with an empty packet of Lambert and Butlers.

Eat chips. Go on MSN Chat
at a mate's house. Download porn.
Blowjobs in the street.
Drink a can of his mate's dad's Heineken.

(Hood in the up position)

Walk home at eleven.
A cold wind. Two days,
then the first GCSE.
He'll wing it like he wings everything.

Bed. Hoodie on the floor
cradling his smells.
Tobacco, sweat, Lacoste.

Harriet Torr

Hospital Room

Light uncrinkles the old man
folded up like a starch image
in his chair, stiff and still as the walls,
remembering himself as he ran free
in the patient fields, bronze as the sun.

Or lying under the roof's quarter
imagining the world's fist engaging him;
smelling the spattered blood on smooth stone
his hero voice crackling the radio waves.

Or owl-fast in a barn's tender
limbs crumbling the hay; his first kiss
when the planets divided themselves
and stars became permanent.

Death of a High-Riser

I stood on the side wings
whilst it all happened, the funeral,
the service, the customary hymns.
People mouthing 'ohs' and 'ahs'
with eyes fixed on a butterfly,
banging its head on the stained glass.

You loved the moors, the wild world
beyond the hills, the happiness of streams,
a cut-out book of memories under a warm sun.
And poppies, their red flags signalling
the wind, catching the butterflies' breath
smudging their pollen to the next town.

Above all, you loved your high rise flat,
the window onto the swarm of the Pennines
and the thick flank of the Medlock River,
the grey slaking of the ceiling
which opened up a map of the world
where you could travel at will.

Seas were nothing to you, one roll
of the eye ball and there you were,
the ancient monasteries of Tibet
peopled in your thoughts
with your latest angels
wall papering the moon.

James Turner

When Buildings Collapse

Who'd be far-seer harping on,
sweatered and fleeced at summer's height
against the coming cold?

Who'd dial a liar merely to seem,
while sunk in some soured-grape
turd-scone scene?

Who'd join the safe-crowd
preserved like curds or powdered and musty
in tuns and tins and jam-jars?

Steam-hazy we may be
from a harm-glut of maul and grope,
panic-prone from past box and flog,

yet, herb-wild
bird-wild
tied to no team,

we'd sooner dance roofless
the seam and sod of this sun-struck planet
and for no fee.

Jenny J. Vuglar

In Time

There was a day when I saw how,
in time, the dead would blacken the sky –
uncalled except by the stirring of a drink
or today, biting into a ciabatta
the light dusting of flour on my lips
tasting like skin.

And more than that, how even
the unnoticed transits we make through this city
become afterwards, journeys;
the street names white in the headlights:
Jerningham, Vesta, Waller. Street after street crossed
until the river winds around a boneyard.

The sky is full of men on ladders
placing silver against silver,
building a long curve
that settles over the roof tops like a rainbow.
Promises, promises. When I am old
my eyelids will droop under the weight.

Joan Waddleton

The Piano

All winter it was there,
four square, sturdy, improbable.

Anklets of lush pasture graced its heels
till sudden rainstorms raised the water table,
left it shin deep in its private lake.

Had he hoped she'd see it, hear it talked about,
recollect familiar harmonies,
be tempted to respond?

Wind and rain assailed once polished woodwork
rattled hammers, stained ivory keys.
Passing cattle peered enquiringly.

No sounds, no tyre marks, no footprints even,
one morning it was gone.
No witnesses came forward.

Eddie Wainwright

Tatiana to Eugene:

a bleeding-heart letter offering
her all. What else could she do,
being so smitten? What should he do

about this silly goose? So Onegin
to Tatiana: nothing. She breaks her heart,
gets over it, as one mostly does

(touch and go for a while, though).
Then, of course, he realises:
Oh Christ, what have I done?

Rushes back with his heart
on fire. Finds what? She's married
someone else, stupid. What else

can a lorn girl do? His turn
to mope, which he does,
perhaps for the rest of time.

What should we learn
before moving on? Never
underestimate young girls?

Never turn a tempting offer
down? Above all, never
write about it, put yourself

about so rashly lest someone
take you for a ride (or,
in this case, fail to do so)?

Maybe the best we can hope
is that such never befalls us, or there,
but for the grace…

We should leave them there:
she with her growing brood,
musing *if only* from time to time,

he looking for a pistol
that makes a clean, round hole.
Will he do it, do we think?

Huw Watkins

At Combwich

mud-luscious, toe-gangling not-what-in
the see-river where big boats once came-
never-again, tin-less, load-less, ore-less
and the mud turns-over-itself or sinks
on-top-of as the water rides-itself-out
and the small boats tied-down-to
poles-up in the changing channel wait
for the see-river to push-the-waters-up
to cover the mud-luscious toe-gangling
foot-sinking up-along-down where every-
one's not, where the little boy was discovered
down-further-in-later, un-mud-lusciously sunk.

Jean Watkins

Sheets

After the thank-yous, the good wishes and the kisses
after the waving as the car drives away
they come indoors, regretful yet relieved
at having the house to themselves.

They separate; he goes to his computer.
She clears the coffee tray, then sits to enjoy
the last cup keeping hot. The satisfying silence
seeps through her skin, her mind reviews.

Her cooking turned out well – wine and talk flowed.
The theatre visit and the outings too. They'd walked
the hills, hoping to see red kites, and he'd been thrilled
when two were sighted circling high above.

She strips the guest room beds, hers first then his
but as she lifts the sheets – a whisper of his skin.
At once she's back to when they danced and danced
tight in each other's arms, some thirty years before.

Her stomach knots, and something like
hunger makes her legs feel weak and strange.
She holds the sheet bunched to her face
breathing its scent, wishing away the years.

Uffington

Bald hills like whales are humped
against a midnight sky. Moonlit,
the ghost-horse gallops across time.

Lyn White

Philosophy and Buoyancy

Your arms are doing the breast-stroke
but your feet run along the bottom.
Everyone else does a perfect crawl,
except one man
who cuts a ripple-less furrow
on his back and asks you
for the meaning of life
as he passes.
Just as you are about to speak,
you know the answer to this one,
you cannot stop;
the undertow seems greater
than buoyancy which is
less than gravity.
Your toes trawl, skinned
by tiles that fall away
into the fluid, maximum depth.
Chlorine fills your throat
comes out through your nostrils
and your reply bubbles up
lost in a gurgle.

Hamish Whyte

Her Laugh

I'm learning the buttons
to press, the words
to say: for instance
'cool crisp linen'
or the way the Scots
pronounce ironing,
a phrase like
'away you go'
sets her off –
that husky, sexy
tarry chuckle, ha-has
steeped in thirty a day,
equally at home in dives
and Lorelei Cottage.

Sheila Wild

Byrd: antiphon for four voices

Is it contrapuntal,
the music
for a hidden chapel,

the perfect fifths
falling like rain
from the eaves,

morning light
lying on the altar
like a cloth of samite?

Margaret Wilmot

Six Things My Father Told Me

"You can always get three more drops
out of a whisky bottle,"
my father said.

"Never clean your brushes in a blend, they need
a Single Malt,"
my father said, lurching

across the studio floor to *Nude Rejects Black Swan*, mixing
a little *Laphroaig* into his turpentine.
"Just pass me a rag –

always keep a rag handy." Of course, I couldn't find one in
the vital moment, and when I stopped burrowing, I only
heard "Never."

"Never what?" I asked, tossing him the rag, but
he was painting storm-clouds now. "Never say never," he quipped
minutes later,

"you never know. Maybe this nude will say yes
someday – my swan is still hoping.
Always hope," my father said, reaching for the empty bottle.

Linda Wilson

Someone, Somewhere

Somewhere between the frozen
apple-and-custard pie and the
mackerel in mustard 'n'dill,
she began to feel like an alien.
The trolley kept swerving to the
right, so nothing abnormal there.

Robots in designer clothes picked
kumquats for a planned menu
and plastic for the freezer.
She picked the fluff from
the corners of her pocket, where
the shopping list should have
been but was on the kitchen table.

She wanted to be lying
beneath a palm tree, fingers
caressing soft folds of sand.
She wanted to be deep in a wood,
rolling naked in a bed of ransoms.
She wanted to be running rampant,
like consumerism,
through someone else's life.

Robin Lindsay Wilson

Soul Mates
(Based upon the 1931 painting 'The Café' by Massimo Campigli.)

in a cross hatched café
with a cold pigeon-shit lintel
laid across our pale foreheads

a glass-topped table reflected
our traditional accusations

we would like to go home

the couple unafraid of sunshine
have a table like a watermelon
and a brassy buttercup umbrella
attracting easy tourist profit

we would like to be them

between their hands they protect
the precious red jewel stolen
from the wise toad king's head

each couple looks like a twin
of home shade or foreign sunburn
the waiters never get it wrong

the amphibian world goes by
but does not croak or splash

we think like dripping limestone
in our hands a wedding ring
but we face the man and woman
who share one timeless smile

after ten minutes of promises
we will stroll the boulevard
wanting something undefined

Janet Wiltshire

Nothing is Happening
Via Cavour, Florence

The police are doing nothing
but standing around;
their car across the road
arrests the traffic.

A pool of quiet holds
a muster of wheelchairs:
their owners sit silent,
eyes raised to look about.

They do not carry banners,
they do not shout slogans,
but show a mild elation
to be permitted to be there.

Peace envelops us:
the bus driver leans on his wheel,
nobody honks a horn
or waves his arms or shouts.

As we run now
to catch our train
we carry a sense that
something has happened.

Owl

We only knew him by his spectral hoot
haunting our dreams, until we found
an image on the morning window pane
soft and precise and ghostly white:
we had been visited while we slept.

We gazed at a spread of angel's wings,
a plumy breast and head and, poised in front,
spiked talons braced to meet the sudden
unseen, unexpected jar.

He must have crashed to leave
so accurate a picture on the glass,
yet not so hard he could not fly away
unbloodied and without a feather's loss,
affronted but still dignified.

He left us with a sense of privilege.

Sue Wood

Esther

I am South, further South than I have been before.

We stand in a kitchen which is not mine although
I live in this house and try for home.
Outside an avocado drops grenades of hard green
onto a bare brown lawn.
The jacaranda tree sheds blooms as vivid as lavender fields
while Esther leans at the doorway, holding my son in her arms.
She sings to him in strange ripples of warm wind and blue ocean.
Her words rock us both and she smiles,
her teeth white, her skin as dark as wood.

I prepare lunch, eggs, a few beans,
making two places at the kitchen table.
Esther smiles again and gives me back the knife and fork.
Taking a rough wooden spoon,
she sits on the step, my son asleep on her back,
'Nkhosizane, I sit here and you there. Then we can talk.'

Outside mynah birds jabber in tongues and I inch
South, further South than I have been before.

Jan Woodling

Between Woking and Guildford

Grey clouds whisper thunder and seduction
I want to read Lawrence
purge the sickly sweet cattle smells
of August stations
uproot the passing drifts of buddleia.

Ragwort poisons.

I want to show my vitality
unroll sleeves of passion
storm your waistcoat
lick off the coal dust
and discover the New Yorker.

All Hallow's Eve

I burnt candles all night
bumped into you in Waterstones
after twelve years
a book launch
The Asham Award for women writers.

You were one, of only three men, attending
lurking in the historical fiction
but I recognised you
despite the hat and the green suit
you still remind me of Kierkegaard.

Once you taught me semiotics
instead of reading the first draft
of my dissertation
and giving me written feedback
you invited me to lunch
asked me to tell you all I knew about Plath.

Once you terrified me
but now you've retired
got your own business.
Tomorrow you're flying to Milan
to sell stamps to a millionaire.
There and back in a day.

I felt excited by my courage to approach you
pleased when you sat next to me
I was convinced that you'd ask me out
but you left after the second short story.
An early flight!

William Wood

Edouard Vuillard

Edouard Vuillard could not have known
When in 1894 he mixed his distemper
And began to paint the large, expressive canvas
"Nannies out for a walk" in a Paris park
That two centuries later in the Royal Academy
London, two well dressed women

In a group of women on an outing
Would file obediently past his painting
Engrossed in talk of lawyers, estate agents
And the problems of selling a house
Giving the works of Edouard Vuillard
Barely a second glance, if indeed a first.

A C Clark

Irish Giant
exhibit in the Hunterian Museum, Lincolns Inn Fields

Seven foot eight in its stockinged feet,
his body shambled in its overgrowth
like an ill-fitting bear suit
he couldn't take off, harmless
as the dwarf-girl's hunching beside it.

He knew himself a walking exhibit,
mass of malfunction distended into fame,
stalked by an obsessive
who eyed up his underpinnings.
He blushed for shame

to think he'd be boiled to his bones
like abattoir render
stuck in a peepshow
along with goblin infants,
prosthetic noses, row upon row

of potted monsters. Goliath
outwitted, his plundered skeleton
towers over petty slingshot,
fathomless eyeholes drowning
his scuppered, decent coffin.

Seals

Slugs slurped on rocks. Salt
your cocked tails - why don't you
flip up and off or deliquesce
to boneless heaps?

If you fall asleep
lying out in the sun like that
won't you lose all

that ooze, baked
to a sliver of indiarubber?
and if you seek refreshing depths
to sleek you in your skins

tight as sausages
what huge seaplanted cabbages,
succulent seaweeds

can satisfy giant greed?
Whole underwater crops
turned to lacework.

Sandfields
slicked in thickening
trails like gum-stuck malls.

Beached - your last meal
slowly percolating -
as the tide rises
you soak ultra-violet

sweated through
sky's widening pores
blister scarlet
face down or

belly up.

Devoted
Bones found in medieval monastic cemeteries in London show overgrowth characteristic of an excessively rich diet (estimated at 6000 calories a day)

Monkbones dripping like candlegrease
wound in the shroud of their excess
speak of flesh plumped on partridges
bellies grown bouffant on beer
a welter of prayer

knees groaning under the tonnage
of piety and plum porridge
voices sweet as saintsday sugar
praising the Giver of bread
and wine

as many oysters as offices
in a Lenten day, legions
of lampreys, carp
fresh from meditation
in monkly stewponds

hours of silence contemplating
their inner men in stillness
worthy of Buddha, girths
to rival Gargantua's, mirth
outrolling thunder

and not a whine or a whimper as they bent
under the burden of calories
sending belches to heaven
God's trenchermen all
never once slackening their duty to

His sacred tables.

Colin Archer is a creative writing tutor in Surrey. A widely published poet, his collection *Renewing the Light*, is published by Peterloo Poets.
Norman Bissett worked for the British Council, mainly abroad, 1964-95. Since retiring, he has had many poems published in small presses and has won several open poetry competitions. President, Edinburgh Writers' Club for the past 3 years.
Pat Borthwick has two teenage grandsons. She and her son were jointly 100 this year and flew to observe the Northern Lights in November to see the biggest birthday candle ever. As well as writing poetry Pat has an active interest in astronomy and has recently acquired a professional telescope.
Josephine Brogan's roots are both Scottish and Irish. She was born and brought up on the east coast of Scotland, and continues to find sources for her writing both in regional speech and in a remembered mix of industrial city and rural hinterland.
George Carle lives in a Highland village called Tighnabruaich which is situated in a picturesque part of Argyll called the Kyles of Bute. He has published three collections and contributed to poetry magazines and anthologies.
Liz Cashdan teaches at Sheffield University Institute of Lifelong Learning and for the WEA. Her first collection was *Laughing All the Way* (1995). A booklet, *Pictures from Exhibitions*, is due from Five Leaves in January 2006.
A C Clarke has been writing poetry for many years. She has been quite widely published, with poems appearing in a variety of magazines (e.g. *Acumen, Outposts, Poetry News, Staple*) and in a range of competition anthologies. Her pamphlet, *The Gallery on the Left*, was published by Akros Press, November 2003, and she contributed to the anthology *Exile/Mërgimtari* published by Survivors' Press, May 2004, which features translations of poems by writers from different cultures. She was awarded a menteeship this year on the Royal Literary Fund Mentoring Scheme, her mentor being Mario Petrucci, and this year also won the Petra Kenney Competition. She is a member and current organiser of a poetry group founded by the late Jean Sergeant, the widow of Howard Sergeant. She lives in Glasgow and is an active member of Scottish PEN and Scottish CND.
Kristina Close has had poems in *Poetry Wales, The Rialto, Smiths Knoll, Staple, The Wolf*. She read for an English degree in her late 40s (RHUL) followed by an MA in Creative Writing, University of East Anglia. In 2003, a poem won the Nottingham Open Poetry Competition. She can speak basic Lithuanian.
Derek Collins was born and brought up in Gateshead, but has lived in Sheffield for 31 years. He is Emeritus Professor of Applied Mathematics at the University of Sheffield: poems and mathematics papers mix in his publication list. His poems are published, in *the ticking crocodile*, Blinking Eye anthology, 2004.
Ann Constable is retired, country woman born and bred. She has a great love of birds, and gardening. She has two sons, and two and a half grandchildren.
Rose Cook lives in Devon. She performs poetry regularly, individually and with poetry performance group *Dangerous Cardigans*. She also co-presented a popular local poetry and performance forum *OneNight Stanza*. Her work has been published in various magazines and collections.

Angela Cooke is a creative writing tutor, and works in ceramics. She has had work published in *Orbis, Envoi, Honest Ulsterman*, and many other top magazines.
John Crick is a retired teacher, and occasional poet. Many years ago, he wrote a short book on Robert Lowell – his choice, along with Thomas Hardy, as the greatest of modern poets. How he envies them!
Clare Crossman lives in Cambridgeshire with her husband. She has published *Landscapes*, Redbeck Press, 1996, and a sequence, *The Shell Notebook Poems*, Shoestring Press. 2004.
Judith Dimond came to poetry through the creative writing course at Kent University, (where she also works) and two inspiring tutors. Published in *Poetry News* and many other journals, her subjects often draw on the East Kent countryside where she lives - but sometimes the world insists on breaking through.
Brian Docherty was born in Glasgow, 1953, and lives in north London. Educated at Middlesex Poly, University of Essex, and St. Mary's College, Strawberry Hill. Widely published in magazines and anthologies; first collection, *Armchair Theatre* (Hearing Eye, 1999).
David Duncombe lives in Derbyshire. He has published four collections of poetry, novels for children and has had a play and short stories broadcast on BBC radio. Prizes in poetry competitions include four firsts. Interests include motorcycles, boxing and marathon running.
Margaret Eddershaw left the UK in 1995 to live in Greece, and since then she has had seventy poems published singly, and one collection, *Spectator's View*, 2002. She enjoys the outdoor life – swimming, tennis, and sitting under her lemon trees.
Penny Feinstein started to write poetry when she retired to Derbyshire after teaching and raising a family in London. She workshops poems with an indispensable group of critical friends. Her poems have appeared in magazines such as *Staple, Second Light* and a Bloodaxe anthology.
Beryl Fenton is in her late 70s. Lives in Sussex. Has had poems published, and broadcast on BBC radio 3, and is hoping to have a pamphlet by Waterloo Press.
Sylvia Forrest's poems 'reveal quirky imagination and unique experience' Diamond Twig Press said on publishing her *Waltzing Off from Hand-Me Downs*. At last she's getting on with her memoirs of cycle-camping with her dad in Eastern Europe: her son would like to read it.
Alan Franks was the winner of this year's Southport International Poetry Competition, and of the 2003 Petra Kenney Award. His most recent play, *Previous Convictions*, was produced at the Orange Tree Theatre, Richmond, this year. He has also written fiction and produced four CDs of his songs. He writes for *The Times* and has twice been nominated for Interviewer of the Year in the British Press Awards.
Berta Freistadt is a Londoner and has written poetry for most of her life. She spends her time teaching, gardening and reading trashy novels. Her collection *Flood Warning*, was published in 2004, Five Leaves, Nottingham.

Ann Gibson is 51 and has recently started an MA course in Literature Studies at York St. John College. She is married with two teenage daughters who provide much inspiration.
R. J. Hansford was proprietor of Crete Craft Concrete Products. Later he worked as a librarian. He now finds poetry more arduous than either.
Chris Hardy lives in London. Plays in blues/rock band BIG ROAD (new CD out see bigroad.net). Published in numerous magazines - *Stand, Poetry Review, Smiths Knoll, Pennine Platform* etc. New collection in preparation. Prizewinner in National Poetry, London Writers' and other competitions.
Pauline Hawkesworth has one published book, *Dust & Dew*, Mitre Press, 1969. Pamphlet from Redbeck Competition, *Developing Green Films*, 1998. Member of Portsmouth Poetry Society. Placed in many competitions, and has poems in magazines. *Parents* (anthology) *Enitharmon, Second Light*, 2000.
Don Henderson is big, bald, bearded. Gateshead lad, 72, but could pass for 71; would be fit and handsome but body lets him down. Grammar school, but not University. Loves reading, most jazz; hates all politicians.
Doreen Hinchliffe comes from West Yorkshire but now lives in London, where she teaches English as a Foreign Language. She started writing poetry nine years ago and is a member of the Thameside Poetry Workshop in Greenwich. Her work has been published in a variety of small magazines and two of her poems appeared in last year's anthology, *the ticking crocodile*.
Jackie Hinden is 76 years old, and spent all her working life in publishing. She has taught creative writing in adult education for over 20 years, and as a very mature student gained an MA in creative writing at Sussex University, which reawakened her interest in writing poetry. She has had short stories published and a lot of words set to music, including a children's operetta.
Mary Hodgson was born in Suffolk, and now lives on the Wirral. She taught English in schools and College of FE., and creative writing for local WEA. Published in various magazines. Two collections of travel poems, *New World* and *Summer World*, published by Envoi Poets.
Marianne Hellwig John is married to the sculptor David John, and with six children, she has been painting for over 50 years, and writing poetry seriously since joining a University of the Third Age workshop in 1991. She finds the two arts complement and feed into each other.
Ursula Kierman has published three poetry collections, the most recent being *House of the Left-Hand Door*, (Slipstream Books, 2005). She has won prizes in many competitions, and has been broadcast on local radio. She runs a creative writing group from her own home in Pulborough, West Sussex.
Wendy Klein is still a competition junkie chasing the elusive collection. She still believes in the curative qualities of dogs, belly dancing and reading aloud. All three are essential to her survival. She takes her inspiration, as always, from everywhere.

Bernard Landreth is a retired civil engineer who has recently completed an MA in Creative Writing. He lives in Carlisle. He has had poetry and short stories broadcast on BBC Radio and individual poems have been published in a number of anthologies.
Gill Learner is a Brummie who moved south many years ago. Her poems have won a handful of prizes and been published in magazines and anthologies including *the ticking crocodile*. She can't resist stationery shops, is involved with Reading's Two Rivers Press, and battles stage-fright to read at the local Poets' Café.
Margaret Lewis was born 1922, in a leafy suburb, but moved to the Black Country in '32. Learnt parsing and analysis aged 8 in Junior Commercial College, central Birmingham. Present interests: gardening, photography, and background to Bible Study.
Asit Maitra FRCS, completing MA (Creative Writing), NCL University. A pamphlet *ZIG-ZAGS*, with Pat Borthwick. In *Acumen, Other Poetry, Anthologies: Norwich OPC (97,02,04), Redbeck British Asian Poetry, 2000,* Macmillan's MASALA *(children's poetry, 05) Blinking Eye PC (04.)*
Gol McAdam is a retired senior lecturer dividing her time between Yorkshire and Kent. She is returning to poetry after a long absence. Other writings include academic texts, journalism, fiction and radio drama.
Etelka Marcel was born on the Continent in 1930, and has been writing all her life. English is her second language. Etelka was also the name of her grandmother, who died in Auschwitz.
Gill McEvoy is the Poetry Society representative for the Cheshire area; founder of the Golden Pear Poetry group; creative writing tutor; quite widely published in the small press poetry magazines and online.
Kathleen McKay was born in Liverpool, and lives in Leeds. Publications include *Waiting for the Morning,* The Women's Press 1991 and *Anyone Left Standing,* The Poetry Business 1998. Recent collaborations with an artist on teeth, and with Finnish writers on water (www.intland.net). Mentor on *Crossing Borders* www.crossingborders-african writing.org.
C.E.G. Manwell is a doctor and smallholder in West Wales. Born in Northern Ireland, lived as a child in the Southern Sudan where parents worked. After boarding school in North Wales, attended Welsh National School of Medicine. Member of the Writers' Workshop in University College, Lampeter.
Walter Nash at 79, going on 80, was once a Professor of English, now deeply retired, lives on the island of Tenerife and writes poems, stories, and books about language and literature, the latest of which, *A Departed Music,* is about to be published by Anglo-Saxon Books.
Shirley Percy was born in 1944 and attended Castle Girls Primary School, Northwich, (where she met Miss Armitage). After University she became a teacher and worked with young children for 36 years. She retired from the Manchester Ethnic Minority Education Service last year. This has given her the glorious freedon to write.

Michael Pooley has been writing poetry pretty well all his life, a hard addiction to a hard craft. he is 58, and has lived in the Ironbridge Gorge in Shropshire for the last 27 years, published fairly widely in small magazines, and still hopes that one day he'll get the best of them all under one roof.

Diana Moen Pritchard was born in Hertfordshire in 1946, brought up in northern British Columbia, lived and worked in southeast England during the 1970/80s, moved to Guernsey in 1989 and is a volunteer advisor for Guernsey CAB. Member of Guernsey Writers.

John Quicke is a retired Professor of Education at the University of Sheffield. He is by training an educational psychologist and has recently been working in this capacity for Rotherham LEA. He has numerous publications, including four books, in the field of education. Writing poetry is a relatively new venture. He has had poems published in *Smiths Knoll* and *Portobello* magazines.

Rod Riesco is married with two grown-up children and one grandchild. He works as a freelance translator. Writing poems since 1994 he has been published in magazines and anthologies. Secretary of Bank Street Writers, Bolton.

Andrew Murray Scott is an Information Officer in the voluntary sector. He is the author of three novels (*Tumulus, Estuary Blue, The Mushroom Club*) and ten non-fiction books. His first poetry collection, *Water Works*, will appear in 2006.

Wendy Searle was born in South Africa. She has lived in London for the past 25 years, although 3 of those were spent teaching English in Seville. Poems of hers have been published in *Acumen*, *Orbis* and a PEN anthology. She has recently completed a play based on the life and death of St Margaret Clitherow.

Gordon Simms lives in France with his wife, Jocelyn. Together they run the Writers' Block, which they founded. He has been successful in many competitions, including an *Arvon* prize in 1998. Many of his poems have appeared in print, and in 2004 two of his plays were published.

K.V. Skene has been published extensively and is a two-time winner of the *Shaunt Basmajian Chapbook Award* (Canada). *Edith*, (poems on Nurse Edith Cavell) was published recently by Flarestack Publishing. An expat Canadian, she lives in Oxford

Lesley Mary Smith studied history at the universities of St. Andrews and Oxford, worked for ten years in broadcast television, and now teaches in the interdisciplinary undergraduate program at George Mason University, just outside Washington, D. C.

Geraldine Messenbird Smith has written all her life; her poems were included in *the ticking crocdile*, 2004. She wishes she hadn't thrown all her old work away ten years ago. Recent retirement has given her more time and zest for writing.

Michael Swan works in English language teaching, but finds poetry more fun. His poems have appeared in many magazines, and have won a number of prizes. His collection *When They Come For You*, is published by Frogmore Press.

Elizabeth Tate is a practising artist who lives and works in the North-East. Her work is ideas-led and covers a wide range of materials and processes from word-based scenarios to sculptural installations.

Maggie Tate grew up in Peckham, London, and worked as a teacher in ILEA before moving to the North East with her family. She began writing seriously when she took early retirement from her job as a lecturer in Drama at the University of Sunderland. She has an MA in Creative Writing, and her work is widely published.
Ruth Terrington finds age helps to prioritise her writing, as she no longer has the energy to gallop about doing good. Publication, and meetings with other writers, put the seal on the pleasure.
Pam Thompson lives in Leicester and works as a university lecturer. She has published two pamphlets, *Spin* (Waldean Press,1999) and *Parting the Ghosts of Salt* (Redbeck Press, 2000), and has had poems featured in magazines including *The Rialto, Mslexia, The North* and *Smiths Knoll*. Her work has also been published in anthologies and broadcast on radio. She is currently one of the poets included in the Wrtiting School run by The Poetry Business in Huddersfield.
Harriet Torr is a philosophy graduate (Lancaster) living in the northwest. She has been published in UK magazines and anthologies, including *Interpreter's House, Frogmore Papers, The Arvon,* and *The Daily Telegraph Anthology, Poetry News* (newsletter of Poetry Society), and was a *Blue Nose* first prize winner, 2001. She is having a sequence of poems in the next issue of Envoi.
James Turner lives in Exeter and has spent most of his life in and out of work as an unqualified library assistant. His first collection, *Forgeries*, was published by Original Plus in 2002.
Jenny J. Vuglar was born in New Zealand but has lived in London since 1979. Published in various magazines and anthologies.
Joan Waddleton, founder member of the Shore Women writing group on the Isle of Wight, came very late to poetry so that any success brings great joy. Her work has been published by *Envoi, Interpreter's House, Seam and South,* also a contributor to the anthology, *Parents,* by Second Light.
Eddie Wainwright taught mostly in higher education, and has been widely published as a poet and critic (main reviewer for *Envoi* for 13 years). Six collections of poetry published to date, most recently *Love and Death* (Lapwing Press, Belfast.
Huw Watkins was born in the Rhondda Valley. Two poetry collections – *Times*, and *Reincarnations*. Was one of six poets in Staple's First Edition series – *Sestet*. Winner of the *She/ITV* short story competition 1992, and a Bridport prizewinner
Jean Watkins was born and grew up in West Yorkshire. Teacher training course at Roehampton, London; taught in primary schools. Married, 3 children. Cared for 2 autistic sons. 1987 Dyslexia course. 1995-2001 English PT degree course at Reading University. 2 grandchildren. Now in her 60s, she concentrates on poetry.
Lyn White works as a librarian at the guest library of a Carmelite Friary in Kent. Her work has appeared in several journals, including *Orbis, Equinox, South* and *Smiths Knoll*. Her poems have also been published in two anthologies, *the ticking crocodile* and *Off the Wall*.

Hamish Whyte, born 1947, is a poet, editor, translator and publisher, with a few pamphlets and many anthologies to his name. He is an Honorary Research Fellow in the Department of Scottish Literature, Glasgow University, and lives in Edinburgh.
Sheila Wild lives and works in Manchester.
Margaret Wilmot was born in California but has lived in Sussex for many (many) years. Sources of interest and inspiration keep expanding but (at present) include the connections based on memory, painting and paintings, places, natural science, people's amazing stories
Linda Wilson lives in Leeds, is married and works with students with learning difficulties and disabilities. She has a passion for writing, gardening, trees, animals, and walking in wild spaces. Her poetry has been published in various magazines and anthologies, and has won a few prizes.
Robin Lindsay Wilson has been writing poetry since the age of sixteen. His work has appeared in many literary magazines and he won a commendation in this year's National Poetry Competition. He is currently working as a lecturer in Acting and Performance at Queen Margaret University College, Edinburgh.
Janet Wiltshire finds writing poems hard work and is constantly being blown off course, but sets off each time in hope of netting that elusive butterfly of an idea that constantly flits out of reach. But she is still trying.
Sue Wood lives in Halifax, West Yorkshire and works as a freelance writer and creative writing facilitator. She has a pamphlet *Woman Scouring A Pot* (Smith Doorstop) published as a winner in the 2001 Poetry and Pamphlet Competition as well as poetry in the *PN Review, The North, Tabla Book of Verse, Mslexia* and Peterloo Poetry Competition Anthologies. She recently won third prize in the Torbay Open Poetry Competition. *Acute Elderly* (Lapidus Quarterly, Summer '05) reflects her work in medical settings.
Jan Woodling is a poet who loves sunny days, playing with clay and travelling. She has recently finished the first draft of a novel about her muse, *The Green Man,* and is looking for a publisher.
William Wood worked mainly overseas for the British Council before retiring early to Sussex to write. He has published a novel, *No Time* (Babash/Ryan) and has minor successes with his short stories and poetry from time to time.